20TH CENTURY
fashion
1900-20
LINEN & LACE

20TH CENTURY FASHION – 1900 –'20
was produced by

David West ⚇ Children's Books
7 Princeton Court
55 Felsham Road
London SW15 1AZ

Picture Research: Carlotta Cooper/Brooks Krikler
Research
Editor: Clare Oliver
Consultant: Helen Reynolds

First published in Great Britain in 1999 by
Heinemann Library, Halley Court, Jordan Hill,
Oxford OX2 8EJ, a division of Reed Educational and
Professional Publishing Limited.

OXFORD MELBOURNE AUCKLAND
JOHANNESBURG BLANTYRE GABORONE
IBADAN PORTSMOUTH (NH) USA CHICAGO

01 00 99
10 9 8 7 6 5 4 3 2 1

ISBN 0 431 09548 5 (HB)
ISBN 0 431 09555 8 (PB)

British Library Cataloguing in Publication Data

Mee, Sue
Linen & Lace (1900 - 1920s). - (Fashion in the
twentieth century)
1. Fashion - History - 20th century - Juvenile
literature
2. Costume - 20th century - Juvenile literature
I. Title
391' 009041

Printed and bound in Italy

PHOTO CREDITS :
Abbreviations: t-top, m-middle,
b-bottom, r-right, l-left ·
Cover tl & page 3l: Emil ©
Vogue/Condé Nast Publications
Ltd; Cover tm, m & pages
14tl, 24t, 24bl, 24r, 25t, 28:
Vogue Magazine ©
Vogue/Condé Nast Publications
Ltd; Cover ml, bl, br & pages
4, 5tr, 4-5, 5br, 6l, 6r, 7t, 7bl,
7br, 8t, 8bl, 8br, 9t, 10t, 10bl,
10-11, 11t, 11b, 12b, 12-13,
14r, 14bl, 14-15, 15b, 16t,
16b, 17t, 17m, 17b, 18t, 18bl,
18br, 20t, 20-21, 21tl, 21tr,
21br, 22bl, 22-23, 23l, 25b,
26bl: Mary Evans Picture
Library; Cover mr & pages 3r,
19b: Lepape © Vogue/Condé
Nast Publications Ltd; Cover
bm & page 23r: Porter
Woodruff © Vogue/Condé Nast
Publications Ltd; 5tl: ET
Archive; 9b: Frank Spooner
Pictures; 12t, 13t, 13m, 22t:
Hulton Getty; 15t, 19t: AKG
London; 19m: George W. Plank
© Vogue/Condé Nast
Publications Ltd; 26t, 27t:
Ronald Grant Archive; 26br,
27m, 27b: Kobal Collection.

With special thanks to the
Picture Library & Syndication
Department at Vogue
Magazine/Condé Nast
Publications Ltd.

The author would like to thank
the following for their kind
assistance:
Aquascutum Limited
Burberrys Limited
National Motor Museum,
Beaulieu, Hampshire

*An explanation of difficult
words can be found in the
glossary on page 30.*

20TH CENTURY fashion

1900-20

LINEN & LACE

Sue Mee

Heinemann
LIBRARY

CONTENTS

The rich employed servants to care for their clothes and their children. Here, nannies promenade in a Parisian park (1907). Their charges could hold on to their trailing caps!

From 1914 until 1918 Europe was involved in a terrible war, World War I. Millions of young men lost their lives.

The 1900s & '10s

The first decade of the century, known as the *Belle Époque* (the 'beautiful age'), was a time of great excitement. The World's Fair held in Paris in 1900 showed off the latest styles and inventions. Motor cars were already on the roads, the first skyscrapers were being erected, powered flight was just within grasp and some predicted that, before the century was out, man would have flown to the Moon!

Lace, pastel colours and tightly-corseted figures were the fashion for women from 1900 to around 1908.

In the world of art, Picasso painted the first cubist painting. The touring Russian Ballet (known as the *Ballets Russes*) set a new, exotic style with its lavish sets and costumes. Cinema was still a novelty, but Hollywood emerged as the movie world capital and the first film stars appeared.

A tour of Italy by motor car in 1900. Only the rich could afford a car; for others, the bicycle was a popular means of transport.

There was political upheaval. Trouble in the Balkans led to the horror of World War I and trench warfare. In Russia, the royal family was overthrown in the revolution of October 1917, which was followed by civil war.

Women gained greater independence, due to the efforts of the suffragettes and because they had done men's jobs during the war.

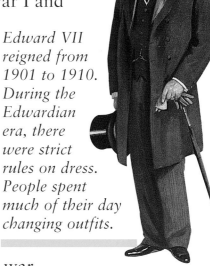

Edward VII reigned from 1901 to 1910. During the Edwardian era, there were strict rules on dress. People spent much of their day changing outfits.

The resulting changes in lifestyle had an enormous effect on the clothes people wore. The elaborate and restrictive fashions, which had mainly been worn by the wealthy, were gradually replaced by simpler, more practical garments.

Rustling SKIRTS

Fashionable ladies glided through the first few years of the century, visions of loveliness in floating chiffon and lace. The look of the time required a small hand-span waist, full, shelf-like bosom and large hips.

CONSTANT CHANGE

Etiquette demanded the right outfit for every occasion, so fashionable people changed clothes many times a day. There were garments for morning, afternoon and evening, and a whole host of outfits specially designed for a single activity such as walking or motoring.

This illustration from 1903 shows a young girl putting on her corset. This gave the desired 'hour-glass' silhouette – tiny waist and ample bosom.

INTRICATE HANDIWORK

Pale shades such as rose pink, pearl grey, soft mauve and eau de nil (a watery blue-green) replaced the dark colours worn by the Victorians. Dull, stiff materials gave way to sheer fabrics, such as chiffon, which were decorated with intricate embroidery and insertions of broderie anglaise or lace. Ball-gowns were often elaborately trimmed and covered with beads and sequins.

LE FROU-FROU

In the evening, necklines were low to show off the bosom. But the sight of a lady's ankle was quite shocking, so skirts were long and very full at the back and often had trains.

Women wore layers of frilly petticoats. These were known as frou-frou, because of the rustling, swishing noise they made.

An underskirt of stiff silk or taffeta made a swishing, 'frou-frou' noise as the wearer walked along.

PIGEON CHESTS

During the day, the body was covered from neck to toe. Boned lace collars forced the head up as a long, swanlike neck was considered very attractive. Bodices were loose, pouched and decorated with frills, or row upon row of pin tucks. The overall effect was as puffed out as the chest of a pigeon!

TAILOR-MADES

Partly due to the popularity of the magazine character the Gibson Girl, who wore separates, suits became popular, especially among independent women. Known as tailor-mades, these were often bought ready-to-wear.

HAND MAIDS

Getting dressed was a difficult business because of all the tiny buttons and fiddly fastenings. Looking after the different garments took up a lot of time, too, so most wealthy women employed maids.

Drawings of the Gibson Girl appeared in Colliers *magazine. Often dressed in a blouse and long skirt, she had the type of figure that most women longed for.*

THE GIBSON GIRL

Stage stars were the pin-ups of the time and postcards of them were widely available. One of the most famous was the American actress Camille Clifford, who first starred on the London stage in 1904. She was known as the Gibson Girl, after a character drawn by American artist Charles Dana Gibson. She had the same, desirable body shape as Gibson's beautiful wife, Irene Langhorne, who was the original inspiration for the Gibson Girl character.

Postcard of Camille Clifford, 1907.

A walking dress (1902) shows the taste for lacy trimmings and the S-bend silhouette.

UNDERCOVER *story*

The fragile exterior presented to the world by Edwardian ladies was not all that it seemed. Delicate, floaty dresses hid heavily-boned corsets and layers of elaborate undergarments. These were necessary to force women's bodies into the fashionable shape of the time, the S-bend.

CORSETS & COMBINATIONS

Corsets had rigid bones to flatten the stomach and create the shape. They thrusted out the behind and pushed out the bust. This shaped the body into an S-bend, so-called because it followed the curves of a letter 'S'. Under the corset a vest-like garment of fine linen or muslin, called a chemise, was worn. Some people wore combinations (all-in-one suits consisting of a chemise and wide-legged drawers). For winter these undergarments were made of wool or silk, while linen or cotton was cooler for the summer. Belted combinations were worn as swimwear, though ladies wore bloomers in the water instead.

PRETTY PETTICOATS

Several rustling petticoats were worn one on top of the other. The top one, known as an underslip, was usually made of stiff satin. Trimmings on all underclothes were lavish and included lace, embroidery and strips of delicate, shiny ribbon.

An early example of the brassière advertised in the German magazine, Jugend in 1915.

Making a big splash in 1909 in an unusually daring combination bathing suit. Most swimmers did not reveal this much leg!

A postcard from 1910 shows the new, longer style of corset. Though not as restrictive around the waist, it kept the thighs clamped tightly together and it was still awkward to lace up. Often, more than one pair of hands were required.

Around 1910 a new, straighter silhouette came into fashion. Long 'drawers' replaced combinations and corsets became shorter above the waist but longer over the hips. As skirts narrowed, petticoats became slimmer and lost their rustling frou-frou.

INTRODUCING ... THE BRA

During the 1910s the bust bodice, or brassière, began to be worn and a less exaggerated shape took over. The bra was invented by Caresse Crosby (her real name was Mary Phelps Jacobs) from two handkerchiefs and a piece of ribbon. She patented her design in the United States in 1914.

THE COST OF CORSETS

Although machine-made underwear was available, much was still hand-made. Those who could not afford to buy hand-made underwear (which was usually more costly) could always resort to making their own. Many magazines of the time such as *Weldon's*, included simple underwear patterns for the home dressmaker.

A 1912 advert for corsets by Peter Robinson of Oxford Street, London.

THE CORSET COMES OUT!
Apart from the odd glimpse of petticoat, underwear stayed firmly out of sight. But attitudes change: during the 1970s and '80s underwear was to be designed as outerwear by the likes of Vivienne Westwood and Jean-Paul Gaultier. The fashion went on to be widely imitated by club-goers. No longer were undergarments coyly hidden, only to be hinted at by a gentle rustle!

Pop star Madonna in a corset designed for her by Gaultier.

UNLACING the stays

During the 19th century objections began to be raised against the fashion for women to be so tightly-corseted. Some people thought tight corsets were unhealthy. Others felt that the rigid fashions simply did not look attractive.

Paris fashions of 1913 featured long, empire-line robes. The looser style freed women from constricting corsets. A gauzy scarf and parasol, or an outsize hat, finished the outfit.

DRESS FOR HEALTH …

In the United States, Amelia Bloomer (1818–94) had promoted practical dress for women since the mid-19th century. Separated skirts called bloomers were named after this fashion pioneer. In Britain, the Rational Dress Society (founded in 1881) also promoted comfortable styles of dress: its members wore unboned stays instead of corsets and baggy Turkish trousers instead of skirts.

Georges Doeuillet's 1912 collection included this flowing dinner gown.

… & DRESS FOR BEAUTY

A group of painters known as the Pre-Raphaelites also challenged the accepted fashions by dressing their models in flowing, medieval-style garments. This look came to be known as aesthetic dress and had quite a following among people in artistic circles, such as author Oscar Wilde (1854–1900) and his wife.

RELAXING IN A TEA GOWN

Despite the various attempts to bring less constricting clothing into mainstream fashion, women spent much of the first decade of the 20th century corseted into the S-bend shape. However, for one short period in the day, before dressing for dinner, they could relax in a tea gown. This was a loose, flowing garment made of soft, filmy fabric such as lace or chiffon, with a low neckline and long sleeves, and did not need to be worn with a restrictive corset.

HISTORY OF LACE

Lace, made from linen, first appeared during the Renaissance in Italy and then Flanders (now Belgium). It was made by hand from linen yarn until the 1800s. Then machines began to be used to make cheap, 'imitation' lace and, in general, cotton replaced linen. In 1900, the chief producers of hand-made lace were Italy, Belgium, France, England, Ireland and China. However, the slow, intensive labour involved was very costly. By 1920 the industry had died out and almost all lace was machine-made.

Lace-trimmed evening-dress by Austrian couturier Drécoll, 1913.

DESIGNER TEA GOWNS

Film stars and royalty headed to top designers for their tea gowns. These included London designer Lucile (1863–1935), Jacques Doucet (1853–1929) and the House of Doeuillet (founded in 1900) in Paris. Garments created by the Spanish-born designer Mariano Fortuny (1871-1949) were also greatly sought after by society ladies. In 1907 Fortuny created the Delphos robe, a simple tunic of pleated silk and he patented his pleating process in 1909. Fortuny's gowns had a timeless quality and are still admired today. They helped to bring about a revolution in fashion that led to elegant, more comfortable styles of dress.

Dresses worn for relaxing at home became simpler and more comfortable, but no less beautiful. This house gown is trimmed in costly fur.

A couple dine in a Fifth Avenue restaurant, New York. By 1917 the female silhouette had relaxed and the S-bend had disappeared.

Dressing for the COMBUSTION AGE

At the beginning of the 20th century there was a growing interest in leisure activities. The most fashionable was 'automobilism' – motoring.

An advert from around 1905 for long, leather motoring knickers, a leather coat and skirt.

BIRTH OF THE MOTOR CAR

The first cars had been developed in Germany in the late 1880s, by Karl Benz (1844–1929) and Gottlieb Daimler (1834–1900). At the turn of the century, cars were hand-made and only affordable to the very rich. All that was about to change. American Henry Ford's first 'Model T' car was produced in 1908. Its standard shape and colour (black), made it much cheaper to make. By 1920, half the cars in the world were 'Model T's. France was another major player, with companies such as De Dion-Bouton, Peugeot and Renault leading the field.

A painting from 1909 shows motoring wear, including beekeeper-style bonnets, goggles and furs.

DAYS BY THE SEASIDE

A popular destination for the wealthy motorist was the seaside, but even the poor got to enjoy the sea and the sand. Public coaches called charabancs took day-trippers on jaunts and excursions. Charabancs were open-top, but these travellers did not have a special wardrobe for the occasion and made do with simple straw hats.

A trip to the seaside in a charabanc, 1918.

Turn-of-the-century English motorists wear goggles and noseguards for a country jaunt in a fashionable French car.

FUNCTION & FASHION

In those days, many roads were little more than dirt tracks. Early cars had no windscreen, doors or roof, so motoring was a dirty, dusty business. Protective clothing was essential! Top stores introduced ranges of motoring clothes for their wealthy customers. Tweed or leather coats were warm for winter; in summer, ladies favoured a dust coat or 'duster'. This was made of silk, which is a natural dust repellent, or linen.

ROAD KILL

Fur was also very popular – adverts for motoring dress included coats made from hamster, squirrel, beaver and sealskin. Even children were wrapped up in furs, with white rabbit-skin being a popular choice. The fashion for fur started in France, considered by many to be the leading motoring nation.

A tasselled motoring hat from 1912. This style of hat was perfect for keeping a hair-style dust-free.

HEADS, SHOULDERS, KNEES & TOES

The motoring craze brought in all sorts of outlandish accessories. Long, gauntlet-style gloves stopped the wind and dust from getting up sleeves. To protect the eyes, there were goggles, veiled beekeeper-style bonnets or balaclava-like hoods with a silicone visor. There were different ways of keeping the legs and feet warm. Gentlemen favoured leather leggings whilst the ladies tended to rely on a fur foot muff (rather like a giant slipper). The travelling rug was an essential item: it blanketed the legs – or cushioned the behind on a bumpy ride!

The changing SILHOUETTE

This printed day dress by Poiret from 1912 shows the new, high-waisted empire line. Such styles gave women much more freedom at the waist.

Around 1907 trailing skirts gave way to a tapered, clinging style, that finished several centimetres higher than before. One of the most influential designers of this new look was French couturier Paul Poiret (1879–1944).

Poiret had a huge impact. The silhouette remained slim and simple, as seen in this dress from 1919.

CLEAN LINES

After a four-year apprenticeship with couturier Jacques Doucet, and a short time spent at the House of Worth (founded in 1858), Poiret opened his own business in 1903. Determined to free women from the S-bend, in 1906 he introduced a simple, high-waisted dress, similar to that worn in the French *Directoire* period, a century earlier.

PUBLICITY MACHINE

Poiret was not alone in this idea, but in one respect he was ahead of most designers – he knew the power of publicity. At the time, only a few customers saw a designer's latest creations. In contrast, Poiret commissioned albums to illustrate his designs.

SWEATSHOPS

Although the sewing machine had been invented in the 1800s, many clothes were still made in sweatshops – no matter what style was in fashion. 'Sweated labour' included women and children. They worked long hours, often in dreadful conditions, and were very poorly paid.

Brochure from the Exhibition of Sweated Industries, 1906.

He used mannequins and made films of their 'fashion parades'. He toured Europe with a group of models and even lectured in the United States to bring his creations to a wider audience.

IMPRISONED AGAIN!

But no sooner had Poiret freed women, than he imprisoned them again. He designed a long, slim skirt that narrowed at the ankle so that it was only possible to walk by taking tiny steps. Amazingly, the fashion caught on and by 1911 was known as the hobble skirt because the wearer literally hobbled along. Some women wore garters that joined the legs at the knee, so that they would not take too big a step!

A hobble skirt by Paul Poiret, 1913. The flared winter coat provided the perfect contrast to the tight, tapering skirt.

At this US Navy League Ball, held at the Savoy Hotel in 1912, dancers twirled in loose-fitting gowns.

FREEDOM FIGHTERS

At the same time that the hobble skirt became popular, a group of people known as the suffragettes were campaigning for greater freedom for women. In particular, they wanted women to be allowed to vote. To draw attention to their cause, suffragettes wore three particular colours – purple, white and green – which stood for loyalty, purity and hope. The suffragette newspaper *Votes for Women* had a regular feature called 'Concerning Dress' which focused on fashion. It also published a list of businesses that provided garments and accessories in the suffragette colours.

THE LATEST SACK-RACE

Many ridiculed the hobble skirt, which was almost impossible to walk in.

COMPLETING *the outfit*

The fashionable Edwardian lady was not just concerned with the right dress to wear for each occasion, but also had to choose from a wide range of accessories. These included such fripperies as swans-down boas and lace parasols with carved handles. But as time went on and fashions became more practical, so did accessories.

STYLISH SHOES

Turn-of-the-century boots were made of kid or patent leather with laces at the front or buttons at the side. Slip-on court shoes were popular daywear, sometimes jazzed up with bows or buckles, whilst for evening, beading and embroidery were all the rage. Louis heels were popular but as the decade wore on, a straighter shape known as a Cuban heel took over. During the war years, practical styles such as brogues (lace-ups of punched leather) came into fashion.

Shoes from 1912, when the Cuban heel was in fashion. Laces, bows and brogue-style holes punched into the leather added decoration.

HIGH HATS ...

For much of the first decade, women wore their hair piled high on the head. For hats, too, the emphasis was on height. Hats were often covered in the plumage of ostriches or gamebirds, such as pheasants, but the most sought-after were 'osprey', which were feathers taken from any exotic species including the bird of paradise. Along with costly furs, rare plumage was something of a status symbol.

A hat from 1900 shows the fashion for brims piled high with plumage – in this case, fluffy ostrich feathers.

... & WIDE HATS

Around 1908 the hats stopped getting taller and became very wide. Such hats became known as Merry Widow hats, after the singer Lily Elsie wore a large hat designed by Lucile for her role in the operetta *The Merry Widow* (1907). As well as feathers, huge, floppy flowers were popular decorations, particularly cabbage roses. For summer, straw hats trimmed with ribbon were very fashionable.

One or two tall plumes, or aigrettes, decorate this hat from 1913. The feathers were usually osprey or egret (a type of heron).

TANTALIZING TURBANS

The exotic, Paris-led fashions just before the war led to a vogue for eastern-style turbans, set off by bands of pearls or gems and usually with a huge jewel at the front. Often, the turban was worn with a single, ornamental feather, known as an aigrette. The war created a fashion for hats with a military air, but after the war more and more women began to cut their hair short and turban-styles came back in.

THE FORMIDABLE HATPIN

From 1900 until the war years, hats perched precariously on top of elaborate hairstyles, skewered into place with hatpins. With such large hats to hold in place, hatpins could be 30 cm long – the length of a ruler! Their sharp, pointed ends were rarely covered and – as many people found to their cost – hatpins could be lethal. Injuries included scratched cheeks and pierced eyeballs!

French cartoon from 1917, when hats were at their highest.

BEADED BAGS

A handbag completed the outfit and might be made from various materials, including beadwork, or stiff leather on a metal frame. Soft, cloth bags (called 'dorothy' bags) with drawstring necks were also popular. From 1910, most bags dangled from long cords. After the war, bags were often fringed as well as beaded, particularly for eveningwear.

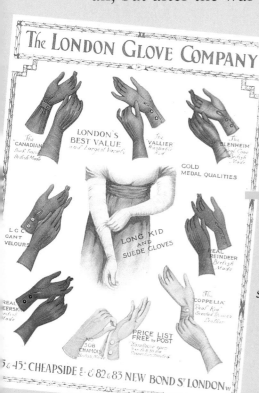

An advert for different styles of glove shows the wide variety on offer in 1912. Deer was a popular choice for soft, supple leather gloves – reindeer, buckskin, deerskin and kid (sometimes scented) were all used. Softer still were gloves in chamois leather or velour.

ARABIAN *nights*

During the early years of the 20th century, theatre had a strong influence on fashion. Designers such as Paul Poiret and Lucile created costumes for actresses and the theatrical effect of these was often reflected in other designs in their collections.

The eastern-style costume worn by the Chief Eunuch in the Russian Ballet's Schéhèrazade *(1910).*

THE SENSATIONAL BALLETS RUSSES

Increasingly, outfits worn for dance also had an effect on fashion. The Ballets Russes, the Russian Ballet company directed by Sergei Diaghilev (1872– 1929), caused a sensation in Paris with its performance of *Cléopâtre* (1909). It starred some of the greats of the ballet world; dancers Vaslav Nijinsky (1890–1950) and Anna Pavlova (1881–1931). The following year Paris went wild over their performances of *Firebird* and *Schéhèrazade*, in which Nijinsky played the part of an exotic, black slave.

BOLD & BEAUTIFUL

The exotic costumes and oriental-style sets were greatly admired and, almost immediately, had an effect on the art, fashion and furnishings of the time. Pale pastels were no longer favoured but were replaced by bright, striking colours and fussy lines gave way to bold, imaginative shapes and patterns.

Like many artists, George Barbier worked in a bold, graphic style in keeping with the new fashions. This piece from 1915 was for the Gazette du bon ton.

A Paul Poiret theatre coat, illustrated by artist Georges Lepape for the art and style magazine Gazette du bon ton *in 1912.*

POIRET & ORIENTALISM

One of the first designers to promote oriental style was Paul Poiret, who in 1909 was already introducing vibrant colour and Eastern-inspired shapes, such as harem pants, turbans and tunic dresses with magyar (batwing) sleeves.

'Lampshade' kimono by Paul Poiret, 1913.

His garments were made from sumptuous fabrics such as satin, velvet and brocade. Poiret made great use of tassels, fur, beads, gilt embroidery and lace. Poiret gave lavish costume parties in order to publicise his designs.

EXOTIC LIFESTYLE

At the time, some people thought that Poiret's designs were totally outrageous but many of his ideas eventually filtered down into the mainstream. He was one of the first designers to think of expanding his business to include accessories and furnishings. Since the 1980s it has become quite common for fashion designers to venture into these other areas with some, such as Ralph Lauren (*b*.1939), successfully offering a total 'lifestyle' look.

An early Vogue *cover of 1916 shows the taste for the exotic: a trailing gown with oriental print and jewelled, feathered turban.*

An illustration by Lepape shows a sumptuous scarlet coat with fur trim. Lepape's artwork style and Poiret's fashions were both influenced by the Russian Ballet.

The MALE image

At the turn of the century, fashion for women was Paris-led whereas men's styles took their lead from London. The Edwardian period – which began when Queen Victoria's son Edward became king in 1901 and lasted until his death in 1910 – was a particularly stylish era in men's dress.

MEN IN FROCKS

Strict codes of dress applied to men's outfits as well as women's. The frock coat, which had been worn in the 1800s, remained correct dress for formal occasions. It was a long, waisted garment reaching almost to the knees and was usually double-breasted.

This double-breasted jacket from 1917 came in styles that were half-belted (as here), full-belted or double-belted.

It was worn open over a waistcoat and with checked or pinstriped trousers. However, to some people, it began to lose favour as it was viewed as rather old-fashioned.

This illustration from the popular magazine the Saturday Evening Post *in 1917 shows the variety of dress styles available to men at the time. With a plain business suit, a tie or bow tie was worn. Country styles featured loud checks or tweeds and knickerbockers were worn in place of trousers and for a sporting look, men wore a tweed cap. From 1916, many of the* Saturday Evening Post's *covers were illustrated by the acclaimed artist Norman Rockwell. The magazine was essential reading for the American man of business and fashion.*

MORNING TO EVENING

Black morning coats were often worn with striped trousers for business wear, although tweed or checked coats with matching waistcoats and trousers were also popular. Lounge suits gradually gained popularity until, by 1920, they were generally accepted for everyday wear. Their jackets were shorter and looser than frock or morning coats. The informality of the lounge suit especially appealed to younger men.

Edward VII (left) in a morning suit. The king was a stylish man. His clothes sense was admired – and widely copied.

Sportswear, 1907-style: white shorts and a sports shirt, worn with lace-up, brogue-style shoes.

COUNTRY COATS

A variety of outfits were worn out in the country or for travelling. The Ulster, a loose fitting overcoat with a large shoulder cape, was popular. Norfolk jackets, belted at the waist and with a pleat at the back, were fashionable for country and sporting activities. These were worn with knee-breeches and the whole outfit topped off with a tweed cap or deerstalker (a 'Sherlock Holmes' hat).

HATS & HAIR

Hats had to be worn outdoors. Silk top hats could be worn with frock coats, morning coats or evening dress. Bowlers (hard felt hats which had domed crowns) and Homburgs (with dented crowns) were also sometimes worn with morning coats. The Homburg was popularized by Edward VII, who often holidayed in the German resort of Hamburg. The king also set the fashion for beards with short, clipped moustaches. Hair was short and manly – long hair was frowned on as it was considered far too 'artistic'.

UNDERWEAR

Underneath their clothes, men wore a vest and long shorts, sometimes joined at the waist to comprise an all-in-one suit. This might be made in plain cotton or in wool. Elastic yarn was not yet used commercially, so socks were held up with garters under the trousers.

An underwear advert from 1917.

A TURBULENT *decade*

The second decade of the 20th century was dominated by the horror of World War I (1914–18). The war had a major impact on most people's lives. People from all walks of life worked side-by-side with the result that attitudes and opinions changed forever.

Women's skirts became shorter and fuller – easier wear for the new jobs they had to perform.

A NEW FREEDOM

During the war women had to take over men's jobs. Often, the work was dirty and sometimes dangerous, for example working in bomb factories. For some, it was their first chance to earn a living outside the home. For others, such as domestic servants, the pay was much better than they were used to. This meant that many women had a little extra money to spend.

THE NEED FOR PRACTICAL DRESS

This new work called for practical clothes. Restrictive fashions such as the hobble were abandoned: skirts became fuller and shorter, until they settled at around lower calf length around 1917. For certain jobs it was necessary to wear trousers – jodhpurs were worn by women working on farms and boiler suits were considered suitable for some factory jobs.

Le Petit Journal

For some women, their only job each day had been flower arranging. When the war came, everyone had to do their bit!

Victoria Station, London, had opened in 1908. During the war, many young soldiers went off to fight in France from here.

Started in the United States in 1892, Vogue hit Britain in 1916. Early covers focused on the war effort.

CUTTING EDGE STYLES
Elaborate hairstyles no longer seemed appropriate, so many women took the plunge and cut their hair short, particularly towards the end of the war. Just ten years earlier this would have been unthinkable!

THE IMPACT OF UNIFORMS
Women who joined the services, such as the Women's Auxiliary Army Corps (WAAC), wore uniform. This had a considerable impact on everyday styles of dress. Military-looking jackets with belts and large side pockets became popular and army colours such as grey and khaki were worn.

WARTIME SHORTAGES
Towards the end of the war there was a scarcity of some types of cloth and skirts began to narrow again. The resulting fashion was called the barrel line, a rather shapeless style in which the skirt curved in slightly towards the hem. The waistline was generally high and loosely belted, creating a barrel-shaped silhouette. Corsets were worn looser or abandoned.

Post-war STYLES

By the time the war ended in 1918 many things had changed. In Britain, some women over the age of 30 were at last given the vote, along with men over 21. During the war many traditional ideas about how women should behave and look had been put on one side.

This practical tailor-made blue suit in gabardine appeared in the final months of the war.

LIBERATION!

Most women gave up their jobs to men when they returned from the war, but the clock could not be turned back. Women had tasted independence and now had more active lifestyles.

AN INDECISIVE PHASE

All these changes had an effect on dress – women wanted to be free once and for all from the constraints of tight skirts and rigid corsets. Fashion went through an indecisive phase, and a variety of styles were tried out in the run-up to the 1920s. A few designers tried to reintroduce pre-war fashions, but without success.

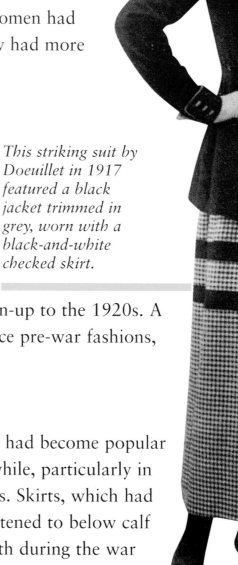

This striking suit by Doeuillet in 1917 featured a black jacket trimmed in grey, worn with a black-and-white checked skirt.

A YOUTHFUL SHAPE

The shapeless barrel line which had become popular around 1917 continued for a while, particularly in coats. Skirts, which had shortened to below calf length during the war years, lengthened again.

Military styling had a huge impact, as seen in this fleecy winter coat, worn with a masculine hat.

HIP STYLES

Then a more tubular shape emerged which continued into the following decade. Necklines often were square or V-shaped and usually collarless. The emphasis was on the hips, in the form of sashes and drapes.

COLOURS & FABRICS

Subdued colours such as fawn, grey and black were worn in the daytime, but in the evening vivid violets and fuchsias came out to play. Evening-dresses featured sheer fabrics over satin or brocade, and gold and silver lamé were also popular. Filmy bodices were often open to the waist at the back and front, and sat over underbodices with straight-cut necklines. Trimmings included fringing, beaded edgings and tasselled sashes.

The checked collar, belt and gauntlet cuffs of this luxurious winter coat from 1918 are in fur: black beaver and white ermine.

DANCING INTO THE NEXT DECADE

Fringing and tassels were perfect dancewear, because they swayed when the wearer moved. Dancing had been a popular pastime for much of the 1910s. In addition to the daring tango, a succession of strangely-named dances, including the 'bunny hug' and the 'turkey trot', had kept dancers on their toes. Even during the war years, the craze for dancing had remained strong and seemed set to continue as a major influence on dress into the roaring '20s.

WEARING THE TROUSERS
The French actress Sarah Bernhardt (1844–1923) had appeared in trousers in the late 1800s, but that was considered very shocking. Then, around 1910, the influences of Poiret and the Russian Ballet led some society ladies and intellectuals to adopt harem pants. After the war, a few forward-thinking women began to wear trousers, but this was extremely rare until the '20s, when French designer Coco Chanel introduced beach pyjamas and yachting trousers for women.

An early trouser suit with turn-ups from 1919.

Fashions of the SILVER SCREEN

During the first years of the 20th century, cinema was still in its infancy. Films were nothing like the sophisticated blockbusters that we see today. As late as 1920, movies were still silent and in black and white. Nevertheless, it was in this period that the very first film stars emerged.

Lillian Gish starred in many of director DW Griffiths' films, including The Birth of a Nation *(1915).*

ON-STAGE STYLE

American performer Isadora Duncan's bare feet and skimpy robes shocked and thrilled Edwardian audiences. Duncan toured Europe widely and helped to popularize less restrictive styles of dress.

Dancer Isadora Duncan (1878–1927).

FROM STAGE TO SCREEN

One of the earliest stars was Canadian-born Mary Pickford (1893– 1979). Like many early screen actresses, she began her career on the Broadway stage. She appeared in her first film in 1909 and earned the nickname 'sweetheart of America' with starring roles in films such as *Rebecca of Sunnybrook Farm* (1917), *Poor Little Rich Girl* (1917) and *Pollyanna* (1920). For these films, Pickford wore Victorian or Edwardian confections of lace and frills.

A STRONG WOMAN

Offscreen, Pickford was a shrewd businesswoman. Together with fellow-actors Douglas Fairbanks (1883–1977) and Charlie Chaplin (1889–1977) and director DW Griffiths (1875–1948), she founded the Hollywood film company United Artists. She also introduced one of the other silent stars, Lillian Gish (1893–1993) to the silver screen. Gish, too, had started out as a stage actress and tended to play sweet, vulnerable characters onscreen.

Mary Pickford played dreamy young girls wearing full, frilly dresses.

SEXY STARS ...

As the decade progressed, women began to take more active, independent roles in real life and cinema-goers were ready for female stars with stronger, sexier images. The new actresses were exotic and vampish. Their kohl-rimmed eyes and beaded, oriental-style clothes drew inspiration from the pre-war Russian Ballet – and became the inspiration for the vamps and flappers of the 1920s.

Polish-born actress Pola Negri wore heavy make-up and jewels, in anticipation of the vampish styles which were to come.

... & WILD WOMEN

Even the names of these new actresses were exotic. Born in 1897, Pola Negri became one of the first European stars, appearing in films by German director Ernst Lubitsch (1892–1947) before making it in Hollywood in the 1920s. For Lubitsch's lavish productions, Negri wore skimpy laces, lush velvets and strings of beads. But the greatest vamp of all was American actress Theda Bara (1890 –1955). Her face was powdered a deathly white and looked even paler because of her red lips and her eyes, which were heavily made up in purple. Rumoured to have magical powers, she kept a pet snake and her stage name was an anagram of 'Arab Death'! She starred in the exotic classics *Cleopatra* (1917) and *Salomé* (1918). For these, costumes included sheer harem pants and patterned silk pyjamas. These daring fashions set the style for wild-living women well into the next decade.

Many top designers created wardrobes for the stars. Mary Pickford's outfits, including this grey dress with matching jacket, were made by the French designer Jeanne Lanvin. Scarlet stitching around the cuffs and collar and a stylish navy blue straw hat complete the outfit.

Actress Theda Bara's revealing costumes ('20) were a far cry from the romantic lace and ruffles of earlier stars.

Even though the process for making the first artificial fibre, rayon, had been discovered in 1892, rayon was not widely used until the 1920s. For the first two decades of the 20th century, fashions continued to be made mainly in natural fabrics. But one technological advance did affect fashion in this period and that was weatherproofing.

IN THE 1800s

Leather and rubber are naturally waterproof, but can be damp and uncomfortable to wear. In the 19th century there had been a race to discover a breathable, weatherproof fabric. One of the first companies to succeed was London firm Aquascutum (from the Latin for 'water' and 'shield') in 1853. Three years later, Thomas Burberry (1835–1926) developed a cloth called gabardine that withstood wind as well as rain.

A Burberry tweed cape worn with a matching suit ('17). War-time shortages made it essential for clothes to be practical.

AT THE POLES & IN THE TRENCHES

Weatherproofing began to attract serious interest in the early 1900s. The clothes made by Aquascutum and Burberrys were ideal for motorists and became high fashion. As well as ranges for motoring and field sports, Burberrys developed special clothing for polar expeditions, ballooning and aviation (flying). During the war, waterproof coats were issued to officers. These provided some protection against the cold and damp of the trenches. Almost a century on, trenchcoats remain key fashion items.

HOW YARN IS MADE
Natural fabric starts life as fluff, whether it is wool from an animal or cotton or flax from a plant. This needs to be transformed into yarn before it can be used for making clothes.

The basic process is the same whether the yarn produced is wool, cotton or linen and machinery used today is little different to that of 1900.

The raw material arrives at the mill packed in bales. These are broken up into fluffy scraps, then fed in to the picker (1). Here, it is disentangled, cleaned and rolled into sheets called laps.

The next part of the process is carding (2). Here, the rolls of rough, loose material are pulled and straightened to make strands or slivers.

These slivers are then combined for strength and stretched out to make the yarn. This is called drawing (3). This process can be repeated to make extra-strong yarns.

The spinning process (4) stretches the yarn until it is just the right thickness.

Finally it is wound on to large bobbins and transported to the textile factory. There it is woven to make cloth or to be used for sewing.

fashions of the 1900s & '10s

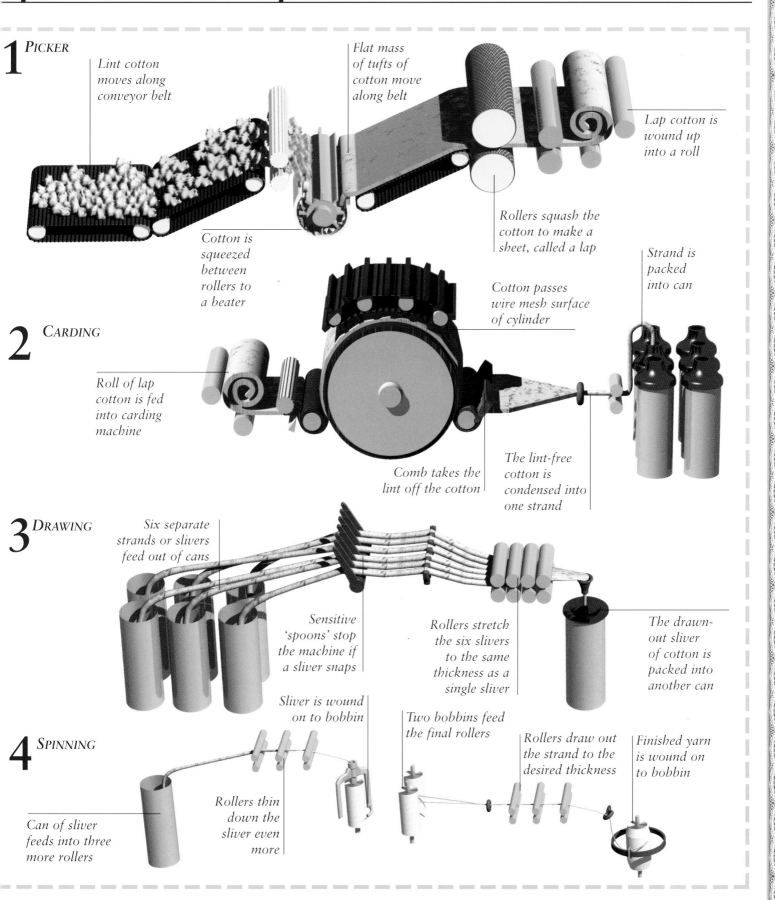

1 *PICKER*

Lint cotton moves along conveyor belt

Flat mass of tufts of cotton move along belt

Lap cotton is wound up into a roll

Cotton is squeezed between rollers to a beater

Rollers squash the cotton to make a sheet, called a lap

Strand is packed into can

2 *CARDING*

Cotton passes wire mesh surface of cylinder

Roll of lap cotton is fed into carding machine

Comb takes the lint off the cotton

The lint-free cotton is condensed into one strand

3 *DRAWING*

Six separate strands or slivers feed out of cans

Sensitive 'spoons' stop the machine if a sliver snaps

Rollers stretch the six slivers to the same thickness as a single sliver

The drawn-out sliver of cotton is packed into another can

Sliver is wound on to bobbin

Two bobbins feed the final rollers

Rollers draw out the strand to the desired thickness

Finished yarn is wound on to bobbin

4 *SPINNING*

Can of sliver feeds into three more rollers

Rollers thin down the sliver even more

Glossary

AESTHETIC DRESS Loose clothing, popularised by artists known as the Pre-Raphaelites.

AIGRETTE An ornamental osprey or eagle feather.

BARREL LINE A style which curves towards the hem to create a barrel shape.

BLOOMERS Full trousers, named after dress reformer Amelia Bloomer.

BROGUE Style of shoe in which the leather is punched with decorative holes.

COMBINATIONS An all-in-one piece of underwear, comprising a vest-top and long knickers.

CUBAN HEEL Short, straight, thick heel as worn by gauchos (South American cowboys) to keep the feet in the stirrups.

DIRECTOIRE PERIOD Period when France was at the height of its power (1795–99) and was ruled by the Directorate.

DOROTHY BAG A cloth bag with a drawstring neck, especially popular from the 1880s to the 1920s.

EMPIRE LINE A style of dress with a high waistline.

FROU-FROU Used to describe rustling silk petticoats.

GABARDINE (1) A closely-woven fabric; (2) Trade name of Burberrys' waterproof cloth.

HOBBLE A skirt style that is extremely narrow at the bottom, popularised by Poiret.

LOUIS HEEL A heel that dips in at the mid-section then flares out at the bottom.

PIN TUCK A very narrow, ornamental fold.

S-BEND Used to describe a woman's figure which has been forced into the shape of a letter 'S' by a corset.

STAYS A corset, usually stiffened with strips of whalebone.

SUFFRAGETTE A woman who campaigned to give all women the right to vote.

SWEATSHOP A place where labourers are exploited because they have to work long hours for poor wages.

TEA GOWN A comfortable gown worn without a corset, so-called because it was worn at tea-time in the afternoon.

FASHION HIGHLIGHT

- *House of Doeuillet founded* — 1
- — 1
- *Costumier Adrian born* / *Drécoll opens* — 1
- — 1
- — 1
- *Fortuny: Delphos gown* — 1
- *Sweated Trades Exhibition, London* — 1
- *Lucile: Merry Widow hat for Lily Elsie* — 1
- *Fortuny patents his pleating process* — 1
- *Hardy Amies born* — 1
- *'Black Ascot': race-goers mourn Edward VII* — 1
- *Poiret: hobble skirt* — 1
- *Lucile survives* Titanic / *Vionnet opens house* — 1
- — 1
- *Brassière patented by Caresse Crosby, NY* — 1
- — 1
- *Balenciaga opens* / *British* Vogue — 1
- *Barrel line popular* — 1
- *Fendi Co founded* / *Lucile closes* — 1
- — 1

TIMELINE

	WORLD EVENTS	TECHNOLOGY	FAMOUS PEOPLE	ART & MEDIA
00	•World's Fair, Paris	•First modern submarine •Paper clip	•Freud: The Interpretation of Dreams	•Death of Toulouse-Lautrec •Death of Oscar Wilde
01	•Commonwealth of Australia established	•Safety razor	•Death of Queen Victoria •President McKinley shot	•Chekhov: Three Sisters •Kipling: Kim
02	•Eruption of Mt Pelée •Boer War ends	•Bosch: spark plug •Lawnmower	•Philosopher Karl Popper born	•Bugatti: Snail Room, Turin
03		•Wright brothers' flight	•Henry Ford founds Ford Motor Company	•Hoffmann founds Wiener Werkstätte
04	•Japan & Russia at war	•First hamburger •New York Subway opens	•Camille Clifford's stage debut in London	•Puccini: Madame Butterfly
05	•Norway independent from Sweden	•Albert Einstein: Special Theory of Relativity		
06	•San Francisco earthquake, USA	•HMS Dreadnought (first steel battleship)	•Josephine Baker born	•Gaudí: Casa Batlló
07		•Hoover: vacuum cleaner •Korn: fax machine	•Baden-Powell founds the Boy Scout Movement	•Picasso: Les Demoiselles d'Avignon (first cubist art)
08	•Olympics held in London	•Ford 'Model T' •Bakelite		•Bartok: String Quartet No 1
09		•Synthetic ammonia	•Blériot flies across the Channel	•Russian Ballet: Les Sylphides, Cléopâtre
10	•Portuguese Revolution •Mexican Revolution		•Death of Edward VII	•Art nouveau 'Tiffany' lamp
11	•Chinese Republic established	•Formica •Machine gun	•Amundsen reaches the South Pole	•Gazette du bon ton founded •Matisse: Still-life with goldfish
12	•RMS Titanic sinks in the Atlantic: 1,500 die	•Electric blanket		•Ravel: Daphnis et Chloé
13	•State of Albania created	•Stainless steel	•Suffragette Emily Davidson dies at the Derby	•Stravinsky: Rite of Spring •Fournier: Le Grand Meaulnes
14	•World War I begins •Panama Canal opens	•Zip fastener •IBM company founded	•Assassination of Archduke Ferdinand, Sarajevo	•Werkbund Exhibition, Cologne
15		•First transcontinental telephone call		•Charlie Chaplin: The Tramp
16	•Easter Rising, Ireland	•Tank invented	•Margaret Sanger opens first birth control clinic, US	•Russian Ballet: Parade •Roald Dahl born
17	•Russian Revolution		•Clarence Birdseye invents food-freezing method	•Theda Bara: Cleopatra
18	•World War I ends •UK: women get vote	•Alexander Bell: hydrofoil •Self-loading rifle	•Russian tsar & his family are murdered	•Gerrit Rietveld's 'Red and Blue' armchair
19	•Nazi Party founded	•Ernest Rutherford splits the atom	•Suzanne Lenglen's first win at Wimbledon	•Bauhaus School founded

INDEX